Introduction

Chapter 1: Introduction

If you're reading this, you're probably curious about meditation, right?

You've been wondering about it for a while, and you keep seeing those inspirational photos and quotes on Instagram.

Those ones saying that all you need to do to get rid of all life's problems is just to meditate. That elusive term which most of us just don't know anything about or understand. It's always that elusive part of society, the vegan meditating happy energetic 'health' bunch.

What is it thatchy do that we don't understand? How do they have this energy, peace and clarity? Well, through meditation of course! But what IS meditation? It looks like it's just doing nothing.

To just sit down, close your eyes, and do NOTHING.

Well, is it true?

Sort of. You can massively improve your life, and more importantly, the way you FEEL about your life by meditating. And for the most part, it DOES just involve sitting down and doing nothing, so how does it work? how can it have such profound effect on us?

The effect meditation can have is amazing. It has the ability to change our DNA making us less prone to Cancer, it can even reduce or reverse depression, anxiety, stress and all sorts of other things. But all of that by doing nothing? Yes. But it's about HOW you do the nothing that matters, but we'll get onto that.

But it won't come easy. Meditation can be a difficult or even uncomfortable habit to build, especially if you've NEVER done it before.

But that's what this book is about. This is to help you start meditating, even if you've never done it before. You just want to get the feeling, and you have some sort of idea about meditation, but it's probably wrong. We'll get onto that later, but first...

How did I even START meditating?

Well, to be honest, I started probably how you did. I was curious, and I just wanted to learn MORE about it. That's how I learned most of the things in my life, I was just too curious!

That's really it.

I read about it, and the thing I've always found, is that if I read or HEAR about something which could improve my life, I'll usually research it. If I research it and find out that it CAN improve my life, I'll ADOPT that habit as my own.

It's the way I become vegan (if you're not vegan yet, you need to research that!), started waking up earlier, started having cold showers and a whole load of other stuff too.

But that's another story. The fact is, I just read an article a number of years ago saying that meditation could improve my brain, make me think faster, help me avoid stress, and slow down the ageing process. I wanted all of that, I mean who wouldn't?

MASSIVE claims I know, but they're all true.

Not only that, but there are dozens of real, proven benefits and effects that meditation has on your brain and body which you probably can't even imagine right now. It all sounds too good to be true, especially when it's just literally sitting down and doing nothing, right?

I felt the same. I didn't know HOW it could all be true, and I thought this has to be a joke. At one point I literally thought that people who meditated were all in one some sort of widespread joke where they would pretend to be feeling amazing but really it didn't have any effect.

Well, several years later, it's no joke. It was all real. My mind has become so calm and focused, I'm able to DECIDE how to react to almost every situation.

People always comment on how calm and level headed I am, and how I'm always able to logically and rationally think and react, even in high stress situations. In situations where the people around me are freaking out, panicking, I'm not. I'm just able to react and decide how to best proceed.

Now, I still feel emotions, of course. Meditation doesn't make you not CARE, it just makes you DECIDE how you react to what you care about, and what you experience.

I still feel and think most of the same thoughts, but I'm able to decide when and IF I want to experience certain things like stress. I can decide if I want to be angry, stressed, sad, depressed etc.

I know it sounds too good to be true, but just go with it for a moment.

And actually, I encourage you to be open minded while you read this book. It sounds insane, and it sounds like a load of nonsense. Especially if you're the sort of person who normally gets angry, stressed, or you just REACT without thinking about what you're doing.

It's hard to imagine something different, or to imagine NOT reacting in that way to something, but it's possible believe me.

I've been meditating every single day for a number of years now. Of course I've had a couple of days when I've not FELT like meditating, but I still did it anyway. I've not become angry or even sad really for the last 6 years or so.

I've still had things happen to me that would make more people angry, upset, sad or whatever. But I can choose to react to the situations differently. I can decide on my emotional reaction, and that's powerful.

Now of course there are other benefits to this, and that's not ALL meditation can do, not by a long shot. First let's just take a step back and think about what meditation is, because the chances are you have the wrong idea about it.

What actually is Meditation?

Meditation is focusing on your breath.

Sounds simple, right?

That's pretty much it. I mean, of course there are lots of TYPES of meditation, which we will cover in detail later but the fundamentals of meditation is that you're just going to focus on your breathing.

While it has existed for thousands of years in every culture around the world in various forms, meditation largely disappeared from the Western style of life until its recent resurgence in popularity.

It seems now for some reason, the Western world is becoming obsessed with the things that most people have known are good for thousands of years.

Things like eating a plant based diet, being ind to one another, practicing yoga, meditating, doing the things you love etc. But only now is it somehow 'trendy' to do those things. And this trend will only grow as people realise their true potential, and realise that they can actually feel a LOT better than they currently do.

For a few centuries in European countries, meditation was even seen as a hallmark of sin, depravity or occultism, largely rising from the practices of men like Aleister Crowley who attributed their self-proclaimed power to meditation and meditative communication with otherworldly forces.

However, meditation finds its roots and value in much more wholesome aspects of life, with positive practices and benefits that anyone can apply.

Literally anybody reading this can meditate tonight and feel the benefits the same day. Of course, you'll feel MORE benefits over time if you practice it every day, but you can get started tonight.

It's used all around the world, by all sorts of people. It's used by various religions, but it's not REQUIRED by all religions. This is probably one of the things that confuses most people about it. People assume that it's LINKED to a particularly religion, or that you have to be spiritual to meditate.

That's not the case.

It's not linked to any particular religion. What's possibly confusing you, is that lots of religions PRACTICE meditation as well as other things. It links very easily with religions and a spiritual practice, but it doesn't HAVE to be used for those things.

Millions of religious people and atheists alike meditate every day.

So let's start to break the illusion that you have to be spiritual to meditate properly. You can meditate no matter what you believe, all you need to have is a desire to FEEL and think BETTER.

That's all. And I can't imagine anyone reading this wouldn't want to feel and think better. Everyone does, right?

Meditation is one of those things when I talk about it that's just a no brainer. I've never had a conversation with someone about meditation and they've said 'Actually no mate, I don't want to feel better, thanks'. Everyone wants more, don't they? More experiences, more happiness, to feel BETTER..

So meditation is just focusing on your breathing, is that it?

Yep. You can choose other types of meditation for example to focus on something in particular, or to change your subconscious beliefs and all sorts of exciting stuff, but for the most part it's just focusing on your breathing.

I know what you're thinking, 'how can just focusing on breathing change my life'. Well, have you tried it? And if you have, have you tried it every single day for more than a couple of months?

It takes about 8 weeks to fully take effect on your brain but you have to practice it every day as we'll explain in a minute. Firstly, let's think about how it actually works and what it DOES.

How does meditation work

Meditation works on your brain by forcing the 'muscle' your brain uses to focus on things to work. It's often very weak, and it's only made WEAKER by social media and a world of instant gratification.

Let me explain:

Anything we want to consume, view or experience we can do it pretty much instantly, just at the click of a button. We tap a few buttons on our phone and food arrives, or even a date.

We can order cars, food, and whatever else online whenever we want. We constantly flick between random videos on the internet, or on our social media feeds.

Most people can't focus on even a VIDEO on social media for more than a few seconds at a time before scrolling down to find another one.

Why?

Because when you watch videos and engage with things like social media, you realise a chemical in your brain called 'dopamine' along with other things.

It's a reward chemical, designed to help us WANT to have sex, eat and sleep. But social media has evolved to make us release it every time we get a notification or message on our social media profiles. So it's addictive, and over time it leads to us just NOT being able to focus on anything for more than a few seconds.

You can see this in almost everyone walking down the street. They're walking in the world but they're looking down at their phones. Or if you're out for dinner and you'll notice people instead of TALKING to the people they're with, they check their phones.

Who are they messaging?

Often they're just scrolling on Facebook or checking emails. But it doesn't need to happen! The problem is that they're not good at focusing any more. Tell those same people to focus on one particular problem for 3 hours at work?

They can't. They'll be checking their phones, emails or browsing random websites within 10 minutes usually. It's tragic, and we're in a real pickle right now in society. People aren't able to form meaningful connections because they're addicted to dopamine and get so easily distracted.

Often people can't focus on ONE thing for more than a few seconds, let alone minutes. People should be able to focus on something for hours on end. That's how I operate, and I know a lot of people who can sit down and focus on something for up to 6 hours or more.

But we've lost that ability over time. We've become like goldfish, running from one crazy idea or thought to the next, without really being AWARE of any of it.

Meditation helps strengthen the part of your brain (the pre frontal cortex) which is responsible for helping us FOCUS.

Specifically, meditation helps you strengthen a part of your brain (a system) called the 'task positive network' or the TPN.

This is the system in your brain which lets you focus on something and engage your higher thought patterns and powers. Higher thought meaning more considered, focused, logical and inspired.

The task positive network is where you want to be operating from. That's where you'll achieve your hopes and dreams, form meaningful connections and live your best life.

The problem is that there's also another system at work in your brain, called the 'default mode network'. This is the system that's active when you're scrolling through Facebook, day dreaming, or getting distracted. It's also known as 'monkey mind'.

It's called monkey mind because a monkey is very easily distracted. One minute you'll be smashing symbols together, then the next you're trying to climb up a wall.

Then you're thinking about that weird sound in the background, now you want to go and watch TV. Then while you're watching TV you get the urge to check your phone so you do that too..

And hours pass this way. Sometimes months and for most of us, LIFETIMES pass this way.

Flitting from one distraction to the next, not really doing ANYTHING to move you closer to your goals in life. Never really DECIDING how to feel, or what to do in your life.

Most people are completely at the mercy of their monkey mind, and that's why they don't achieve success. But that's another topic. Relating to meditation, by meditating you DECREASE the activity of the default mode network, and INCREASE use of the task positive network.

Your task positive network (TPN) however, is your friend.

That's the network that lets you think 'ACTUALLY, I'm not going to get angry right now, I'm going to react calmly.. Maybe this guy had a bad day, or maybe he didn't seem me in his rear view mirror'.

And it saves you a fight. Or road rage, or whatever..

Or maybe the task positive network makes you think 'WAIT, I'm not going to play video games tonight, because I always do that. Instead I'm going to focus on writing this book, or working on this project that's due'.

The task positive network is your friend.

And meditation helps you with that. If I didn't meditate, it would be pretty hard to write this book. At least, the OLD me would have had a hard time. I would have maybe had the idea of writing a book, but it would be LOST in the sea of other thoughts and distractions.

Things like 'watch tv, play video games, make some more food, go to the pub' etc. Success is dependant on the ability to DELAY gratification. It's always going to be more appealing and more fun to just watch TV right now, but it won't get you closer to your goals.

So meditation helps you think differently about that sort of thing. But even if you don't have big life goals, or you just want to use meditation to feel better and relax, it's great for those things too.

So, daily meditation increase activity in the task positive network, and makes you less lazy. Right. But it does a bit more than that actually.

What effect does it have on your brain

Not only does meditation help you focus on the right stuff, but it makes your thought patterns faster, stronger, and more in your control.

The 'fight of flight' response is the reaction most of us have to a stressful situation. In the past it was VERY useful, for example if we see a Tiger, we don't have time to think about it, we just need to RUN.

And in the past, this fight or flight response was critical for keeping us alive.

But today? Well, there aren't many tigers roaming the streets, and the worlds a lot safer in general. Most of us don't experience danger every day.

However, most of us sadly use the SAME fight or flight response when they experience petty, pointless stress like road rage or arriving late to work.

We've somehow managed to evolve to the point where we get stressed on an emotional and physical level, by things that really don't matter and DON'T affect our chances of survival at all. Things that really shouldn't have any effect on our emotional state and certainly not on our physical bodies and systems.

Remember, the fight or flight response has it's place. If you're in a street fight or there's a natural disaster, yes you need that response. You need to be able to react, and move fast in order to protect yourself from harm. And it will be there for you when you need it.

But most of us are reacting to an angry boss at work in the SAME way physically that we'd react to a vicious bear attacking us!

The same hormones, stress responses, chemicals and processes are happening in our bodies in this situation! This means our bodies are experiencing more stress than ever before, because we've lost touch with our ability to be in our BODIES and not our MINDS.

By being so focused on our minds, and our thoughts, we've lost the ability to be in our bodies.

If we were in our bodies, your angry boss wouldn't matter at all. You'd probably laugh at how angry they're getting, I know I sometimes do! It's almost silly how angry people get at seemingly pointless or insignificant things.

Now what do you think the result of that stress is on our body?

When you experience the fight or flight response, your body pumps hormones like adrenaline and epinephrine through your veins. Your lungs expand and take in more oxygen and if you perceive the stress the STILL be there after a few seconds, you get even more.

It's like a gas pedal being held down while the car isn't moving. After a while it burns the engine out, so now imagine the effect of that gas pedal being held down in your body for YEARS on end. It's not good, I'll tell you that for free.

It's actually very bad for your body and mind and over time, it can make you sick. And it does! Chronic stress, which is stress experience in little amounts over a long period of time can make your immune system weaker. Think about this the next time you're angry at someone cutting in front of you in traffic..

By getting angry, you're LITERALLY making yourself ill.

It's quite funny to think about this. We're one of the most intelligent species (apparently) on the planet, and we for some reason choose to make ourselves ill and stressed because someone cut in front of us in traffic for a split second.

It's crazy. We've become blind to what we're doing.

Or, we'll get angry if the waiter brings us the wrong food by accident. This is how we actually behave in the world today!

We choose to experience this stress, and it IS a choice. when you learn about meditation, and once you've read this book you'll have the choice of how to react to situations like that.

The fight or flight response interestingly, uses that same 'default mode network' (DMN). It involves the amygdala, and produces hormones that flood your body with rage, energy and so on. It's useful for an ACTUAL fight or a situation in which you NEED to sprint to get away from danger..

But it's pointless, and actually HARMFUL to have that same response when your boss shouts at you, you're late for work, or the waiter brings you chips instead of soup.

So the fight of flight response is not needed for 99% of our lives. We certainly don't need those stress hormones pumping through our body and not being used to run. It's very harmful.

So, specifically, mindfulness meditation can actually shrink the part of your brain responsible for 'fight or flight' responses, which tend to be more emotional and NOT thought through..

While it also strengthens your higher brain functions which happen in the frontal pre-cortex. This means you're more able to think on a higher level about things logically and reasonably.

This means our normal responses to stress that we can't seem to control, are completely different. We're able, after just 8 weeks of meditation, to have MUCH greater control over our thoughts and emotions in times of stress.

And this really works, I've managed to avoid almost all stress in my life for the years I've been meditating. And the great thing about that is that I've barely NEEDED the stress response at all.

There was only a couple of times when I've actually needed the fight or flight response. One example of that, was to avoid an oncoming motorbike in Asia, and for that situation here's what happened:

My brain notices the oncoming bike before I've really realised what's happening consciously. A distress signal gets sent to my amygdala (in the default mode network, remember?).

The amygdala works out that I'm in danger, and instantly sends a distress signal to my hypothalamus. That area of the brain is sort of like a command or control room. It decides how to act and it does all of this in tiny fractions of a second. It's incredible.

At this point in time, imagine the bike is moving towards me in slow motion. So slow in fact that I'm standing still and the bike just moving towards me a few centimetres a second.

The hypothalamus then decides there's a danger, and it needs to act now. It sends signals to the automatic nervous system telling it to release energy in the body in the form of epinephrine (a type of adrenaline).

This acts like a bolt of lightning, instantly giving energy to the body and enabling it to move and react incredibly fast. My heart starts beating faster, my blood pressure increases, and my lungs expand to be able to take in more oxygen.

My sight sharpens, and blood flows to my legs and arms, transporting the epinephrine to them. The bikes still moving towards me but it's barely moved at all. Imagine a bolt of lightning traveling in slow motion from my head down to my thighs.

I jolt my leg down and push against the ground, propelling me backwards and out fo the way of the bike. The bike passes and I'm safe. This happened within fractions of a second, and it saved my life. Our brains are incredible but the story doesn't end there.

After the bike's passed and the danger's gone, my brain activates the HPA axis. This consists of the hypothalamus, the pituitary gland, and the adrenal glands and it helps to determine if the dangers passed yet or not.

My brain determines the threat is over, and pumps the brake pedal which is the parasympathetic nervous system. It acts as a dampening brake and stops the body remaining all amped up. It helps to remove the stress hormones from my body and has the effect of what we know as 'calming down'.

And the world goes back to normal.

BUT, that's not the end of the story for most people. That's a HEALTHY fight or flight response and it saved my life. But for a lot of people, they REMAIN in that initial stressed response, because their brains continue to perceive their situation as a threat.

This means the hormones remain in their system, and they stay amped up with high blood pressure and so on. Maybe you've experienced a situation where you're so annoyed, angry and stressed that you just can't sit still. You FEEL it flowing through your veins, right?

That's the hormones your brain is telling your body to give you, because it thinks you're in DANGER! It thinks you're about to have a fight or run for your life and it's supplying you with these hormones to give you energy.

But if you don't use them or need them, the effect they have on your body is very harmful. To be honest, you probably have some idea that it's not a good thing to stay all jumped up and energetic for so long, right?

Anyway meditation helps you reduce that, so that you only get those stress hormones when you really need the to save your life.

You won't catch me getting worked up over a meal that's late, or somebody cutting me off in traffic. It just won't happen because I value my health and mental and emotional state WAY more than that.

But there are other things meditation does to your brain as well. It can actually help you experience LESS pain. How?

In the brains of advanced meditators, the pain centres of the brain actually light up MORE, but the people REPORT FEELING less pain. How can that be?

It's a paradox, but it seems that meditation somehow helps people experience less pain. It does this in a very complex way.

The way it works, is that mediators have actually decoupled (weakened) the link between the anterior cingulate cortex (area of the brain responsible for unpleasantness of pain) and the prefrontal cortex..

That means they still feel the pain but it's much less.

The effect of pain in most people, in largely in the mind. There is some nervous system pain which is unavoidable, but the rest of the 'pain experience' we've all come to know is made up in the brain. It's a response to the real pain, and it can make it up to 10 times worse.

In a lot of people, there is a loop which means you constantly re-experience the same pain. But in meditators, this loop is mainly closed down. They're still aware of the pain, but it's much less than non meditators.

Amazingly, this effect can be seen even when people aren't meditating, meaning the meditation has caused a permanent change in their brain and the way they experience pain.

This also applies to the lowered stress response. It seems meditation can physically change the brain for the better in just a few weeks.

Now imagine having meditated for decades. It's no wonder that buddhist monks are able to focus for days on end, seemingly be immune to pain, and even have control over their entire immune system and the intricate processes in their bodies. I don't know if you've seen the videos of the devoted buddhist monks able to channel pain and strength around their bodies. One such video showed a monk resisting a sharpened spear to the throat simply by the power of intention and meditation. Now that's taken YEARS to get to that point, but not everyone can get there.

Why Practice Meditation?

Well, after reading all that, you should want to practice it just to see how it works and to get those benefits.. But we'll explain a bit more about it here. Meditation bestows a host of benefits on its practitioner from the very first.

Some are fairly obvious, like increased awareness of one's own mind and body. Others are often touted but sometimes not clearly explained, like relief from anxiety, depression, panic attacks and other mental illnesses.

Perhaps this is due to a hesitance to accept non-western medicinal approaches to these things, though they are growing in popularity as healing skills, with both the medical community and the world at large.

Meditation can also increase your energy and focus, help you change your behaviours, and improve your quality of work and exercise. It can even improve your immunity and overall health.

Meditation Health Benefits

As described before, there are so many ways in which meditation improves mental health. It can assist in treating mental illnesses like depression and generalized anxiety disorder.

Additionally, it can ease the chronic stress and distractibility most modern people struggle to master. Focus at work increases, and relationships with others improve.

It allows you to build better connections and really listen and care what someone's saying. In short, meditation allows one to be relaxed, present, patient, and grow in wisdom and faith.

Mindlessness, stress and anxiety are shown to damage the immune system and slow the recovery of injuries. They also slow the progress of weight loss, strength training and learning. A mind at peace is a mind capable of just about anything. Working to practice mindfulness pays huge dividends. Here are just a few other things you'll experience:

Better sleep: Meditators are able to sleep better and relax deeper. This can lead to all sorts of interesting effects, like lucid dreams (being able to control the dreams and decide what to dream about) and decreased nightmares.

Improved focus: Of course one of the biggest benefits of meditation is being able to focus on things for long periods of time, and at an intense level. This is massively helpful if you're trying to achieve something or anything in your life.

Increases grey matter: The brains of meditators are shown to actually have more grey matter. Grey matter is like the bond that holds the brain together, and helps it fire signals and process information. The more grey matter you have, the faster and better your brain operates.

Helps you get into flow state: Have you ever been writing something and you just get into the 'zone'? Or maybe you've been playing a sport of working out and you just get into that headspace that's unshakable and unstoppable. You're working faster, better, and more focused, and you don't notice the time passing? That's 'flow state' and meditation helps you get there more easily and more often.

Reduced risk of disease:

This is actually something I want to explain a bit more about. Meditation has the ability to lengthen what are known as 'telomeres' making you resistant to all sorts of diseases like Cancer and Alzheimers!

Telomeres are like the 'protective caps' on the end of your chromosomes.

But wait, what's a chromosome?

A chromosome is essentially a thread of protein and DNA found in the nucleus of our cells. It's pretty important.

On the ends of our chromosomes are telomeres. A telomere is like the protective plastic cap on the end of a shoe lace. It stops it fraying and going all horrible. So telomeres stop our chromosomes getting stuck together and fraying, so to speak.

Over time though, our telomeres (protective ends of our chromosomes) get SHORTER. This

*means that sooner or later, our chromosomes
are no longer protected and are not able to
divide or heal themselves any more.*

**This leads to the cell DYING, mutating
(cancers) or changing.**

And this is how ageing happens, our telomeres
become shorter and shorter to the point where
they can't effectively protect our chromosomes
any more. So our cells start dying.

This is the natural ageing process, but it can be
slowed down MASSIVELY by meditating.
Meditating actually lengthens your telomeres,
meaning your chromosomes are much more
protected for longer.

Years longer. It's like giving your individual cells
a suit of armour to protect them against the
passing of time, and ALL you need to do for that,
is to sit down and do nothing for ten minutes a
day! Still sound like too much effort?

**This means less cells die or mutate, so you
look and feel younger.**

But it's not just about feeling younger though.
When telomeres get too short and the DNA is left

exposed, it can mutate or fuse to other things. Things that it shouldn't fuse to. They can become damaged. It gets dangerous, because it can actually cause things like Cancer and other diseases.

So there are a number of things that meditation can help you with. It can lengthen telomeres and make you more resistant to things like Cancer and ageing. It does this by increasing telomerase activity, which helps lengthen the telomeres attached to your DNA. Powerful stuff.

But more than all of those benefits, comes the feeling of.. FEELING better! Just feeling good in every day life, and not having to worry about the stresses life or the negative aspects of life. It makes you feel good, and for a lot of people that's the most important thing. The increased focus, better sleep and immunity come as a bonus.

The Main Categories of Meditation

Meditation can be approached in lots of ways. There's no one right way of doing it, but there are a few methods that work for MOST people.

Should one type of meditation lose its luster over time, or routine accidentally slip into mindlessness, there are dozens of other ways to meditate that can be familiar to the type you already know or seem totally fresh.

All types of meditation are intricately interrelated, but can be sorted generally into five major categories for an easier review.

These five kinds are: spiritual practice, meditation in motion, visualization meditation, verbal meditation, and Awareness meditation.

But don't worry about those for now.

To be honest, most of them aren't needed. I personally only really use basic meditation technique every morning, and I find that's more than enough to get the results I want. I feel like it's enough for me, but if you want to learn more about meditation and take the practice further, we'll cover that in detail later.

How *to meditate for the* FIRST *time*

How to meditate for the FIRST TIME!

For now, we're going to talk about how to meditate for the very first time, even if you've never done it before. This is why you're here, and you'll be happy to hear that it's a LOT easier than you think to get started.

You can actually get started right now, wherever you are.

Even if you're not at home, there is a way for you to start meditating even while walking around! It's easier to do at home when you're completely relaxed but you don't have to do that. Sometimes I meditate while cycling! It can be done anywhere as we'll explain.

What to actually DO (step by step)

1: Find somewhere comfortable

You ideally need to find somewhere comfortable to meditate. You'll have much better results if you do this somewhere you feel at home and relaxed, but of course, you can do it anywhere.

Try and find somewhere you won't be interrupted, as interruption can be very annoying for your practice.

I've found that if I'm interrupted halfway through meditating, I lose the benefits for that session and can't easily get back into the relaxed state of mind. I have to completely start again, and it takes more time.

So make sure to find somewhere you're not going to be interrupted or interfered with. This can also include things like your phone, noises, lights and other interruptions that might not be obvious now. Put your devices on silent and turn your phone over you the light doesn't interrupt you either.

Also, make sure you've gone to the toilet and you don't need anything. Have a sip or two of water so you're not thirsty during the meditation. It's important to drink enough water during the day by the way! Don't forget.

2: Sit down, ideally on a cushion

Find something to sit on, but ideally, a chair or a cushion. The reason lots of people choose to meditate on the floor sitting cross legged, is because you want to avoid daydreaming and sleeping.

It's much easier to day dream or sleep if you're sitting with your whole body supported by a chair or laying down in a bed. And so a lot of people find themselves just falling asleep, or drifting into fantasies and day dreams when they sit in comfortable places like chairs where their body is supported by the back of the chair.

So try and find something like a cushion, or just sit on the grass outside. That's the main place I love meditating, just a grassy field or a park or something like that. You'll feel better doing this outside as well, as long as the place you're doing it is peaceful and calm.

If you live on a dodgy council estate for example, the park might NOT be a relaxing or safe place to meditate!

But if you live near a deserted lake or something, and there's hardly anyone there, then you can meditate there. I used to meditate in a beautiful meadow in my lunch breaks at work, and there was literally nobody there most of the times I did it. But the one time somebody passed through talking on their phone, it ruined my relaxation mindset.

So find somewhere that you're not going to be distracted or interrupted.

The goal when you sit down is to keep your BACK straight and upright, and your chest out. This lets you breathe deeply and fully, and doesn't restrict you in any way.

It also helps you to relax but doesn't let you fall asleep or drift. Also, make sure you Do actually breathe deeply but don't force it. Just breathe as deeply as you can comfortably do!

It's easy to drift and not focus when you're sitting in a chair, and it's important NOT to do that. To start with, you can use a chair if you have to, but you want to progress to a cushion as soon as you possibly can. It's much easier when you don't have anything to support your back anyway, as you'll discover.

3: Set an alarm on your phone

You need to set a timer on your phone, otherwise you could be meditating for hours. Actually, at the start, the problem you'll have is that you'll try and STOP meditating before it's even been 5 minutes. You need a timer to tell you that you're not done yet!

Set a soft alarm or tone on your phone to go off after about 10 minutes. You might have to start with a lower time like 5 minutes if you're not used to this, because it is hard at first. Like we said about the default mode network, it's called 'default' for a reason. It's the system you most often use, and it's powerful.

So after a few seconds of doing 'nothing' your DMN starts to play up and makes you think about all sorts of things. You'll start freaking out or thinking about all the things you need to do today. So set an alarm for 10 minutes, and tell yourself you're not going to STOP meditating until the timer goes off.

Be strict with yourself because otherwise, you'll only do it for a few seconds. You need to start flexing that meditation muscle and you do that by setting a timer and sticking to it.

4: Close your eyes

If you're doing this during the day it might actually be difficult to keep your eyes closed.

Especially if it's a really bright day and the suns shining down into your room. If that's the case, you can do this with your eyes open but you can't move them or focus on something in your room.

If you can't close your eyes, practice looking or gazing at a spot on your wall but NOT moving your eyes around.

Don't look at the details, just let the object fade away soy o can't really notice it any more. An easy way of doing this at first is to just stare at a candle flame. A candle flame is amazing in the sense that it has the ability to relax your mind and help you just focus on nothingness.

But ideally, you should close your eyes so you can get the full benefits of this. It helps to rcstrict the light coming into your room if you're doing this at home. Over time, you'll get used to closing your eyes for long periods of time so you'll be able to do it in the middle of the day in a park for example.

5: Get comfortable and sit up straight

Make sure you're comfortable and sitting with your back straight. This is a good time to make sure you're not uncomfortable or sitting on anything sharp! Make sure your back is straight but not forced. It should feel quite nice to straighten your back and hold it straight, but if you're not used to doing that or you have poor posture then this might feel a little unusual.

6: Focus on breathing

The most important step! This is where you start the meditation practice. focus on your breathing. That's all you need to do is just focus on how your breathing feels.

Just be aware of your breathing, and experience how it feels, how it sounds and how it must look for your chest to move in and out while you're breathing.

This is where most people fail at meditation, but bear in mind you can't really 'fail'. You can just lose focus for a moment and it's at those moments that you need to bring your focus back to the breathing.

All you're going to do is use count your breathes from 1 to 10. Count 1 with the 'in breathe', then 2 with the 'out breathe' and so on. When you get to 10, start again at 1.

That's literally all you need to do, but to be honest you don't even need to count them. Counting breathes is just a good way of getting beginners to focus on their breathing by giving them something measurable to focus on.

If you're able to, you should just try and be aware of your breath. That's all you need to do is just be aware of your breath.

7: Bring attention back when it wanders

Your mind will wander now, as you focus on your breathing. This is very normal, and a lot of people beginners and advanced meditators have this problem from time to time.

It's easy to lose focus and start thinking about a million other things. But don't beat yourself up about it. It's going to happen. You're going to lose focus, the real growth happens when you NOTICE you're having these thoughts, and then move your attention back to the breathing.

It's essential that as soon as you realise something's wrong and you're focusing on a particular thought, you bring your attention back to just thinking about your breathing. Let's say you're breathing and counting your breathes and you start thinking 'This feels nice, I wonder what happens next? Oh that reminds me I need to leave a review for this book online' and then BANG!

You've lost focus.

But as long as you instantly realise that you've lost focus, and bring your attention back to thinking about your breathing, you'll be fine. That's the point of meditation is being able to bring awareness and focus back to one particular thing or point. In this case, that thing is your breathing.

8: When you finish..

A really important part of meditation is when the timer goes off. When your timers done and you've done your 10 minutes of meditation, EVERY time you finish meditating you need to ask yourself 'how do I feel?'.

This helps you stay motivated.

The chances are the first few times you'll feel a bit nervous or annoyed and it might be a little uncomfortable. This is because your brain likely hasn't done this before and it's weird to have experienced a period of ten minutes where you're NOT thinking about 1000 different things.

But after a while, maybe even the first time, you'll start to feel really good. It won't be like a sudden event, or a sudden 'clicking' moment..

But it will feel good. You'll finish meditating, ask yourself how you're feeling and you'll think 'oh, I actually feel really good.. Really relaxed and happy'. And that's the feeling you should focus on. That's your reason for doing this, and you need to keep that reason in the front of your mind.

What it's going to feel like

A bit strange.

It's going to feel strange. Because you've not done this before (or at least, most of you won't have), it's unusual. Actually, it could feel like any number of things to be honest. Meditation is a powerful tool, and if you've never done it, it can clear emotional or mental blocks you've had for years.

Some people I know start crying uncontrollably when they first meditate, because they've never experienced that sense of calm and serenity. It lets you step back and FEEL your body once more. It lets you step away form the thoughts and monkey mind chatter that's so controlling and manipulative in our lives.

So you might cry, you might laugh, you might feel good or uncomfortable or you might feel nothing at all. The first time is always the most unpredictable.

I think the thing most people experience, is just a sense of calmness and also a sense of it being uncomfortable or hard to concentrate for the first few minutes.

Whatever your experience of meditation is the first time, just accept it.

It might not be what you're after, it might be better or worse. But the truth is after a while, it will get easier. You will be able to access deeper states of relaxation and serenity. It might take you a few days, weeks or even months, but it will happen.

If you keep meditating every single morning and evening you'll feel better. That I can tell you for a fact. I've never met anyone who's meditated

every day for more than a month and felt
WORSE. It's always better, always deeper, more
calm, and they've always found it easier to focus.

Before we go on, make a commitment to trying
this for 30 days. Once a day for 30 days and
THEN decide how you feel. Because otherwise,
you might not 'get it' until two weeks in, and if
you give up the first try or even the second time,
you miss out on the life you COULD have!

Be a little bit patient with this and just give
yourself a chance to really experience it. It might
take longer than you wanted, but stick with it, I
promise it gets easier.

On the other hand you might be reading this
thinking 'it's fine, I did it with no problems!'.
That's great! but for the people who might be
having problems, let's address some of the most
common issues people are going to have with
meditation.

Common problems people have

1: Mind is racing

Lots of people when they first try the technique
just described, report their mind was RACING.

They were unable to think about just one thing, and instead they focused on everything. Their body and how it felt, their phone, thoughts about what to have for dinner or what to do tomorrow.. Everything.

That's really common, and for a lot of people it's just a prime example of how the default mode network operates. It's designed to get you to think about various different things and constantly get distracted. It's attracted to novelty and distracting things like TV shows and instant gratification.

There's not really an easy fix for this, you've just got to power through and build the muscle slowly. Think of meditating like a physical muscle, you can't lift a heavy weight on day one, can you? So don't try and meditate PERFECTLY the first time.

Just focus on doing one thing:

Every time you NOTICE yourself thinking about something else, try and gently move your focus back to your breathing.

After a while of doing this, (this is why you should try for at least a month) it gets easier.

Suddenly you don't think about that other stuff as often, and when you DO, it's easier to move your focus back to your breathing.

2: Falling asleep

A really common problem people have when they try and meditate first thing in the morning is they fall back asleep! If you also get up early, it's super easy to just go back to sleep if you're all warm and comfortable in your chair or laying in your bed.

But that's why it's important to NOT sit in a chair or lay on a bed. If you're having trouble staying awake while doing this, you need to sit on a cushion on the floor, with your back straight.

This means you can't fall asleep even if you wanted to. A lot of people actually THINK they're meditating and feeling relaxed but they're really just sleeping in their chairs!

Meditation is NOT sleeping, it's quite the opposite. It's the act of DECIDING to sit there, AWAKE, thinking about nothing.

But you can't do that if you're falling asleep in your chair every two minutes. So start on a cushion. You can also just sit cross legged on your bed actually, and that's probably easier for a lot of people than finding a cushion and balancing on it.

3: Can't sit down for long enough

Probably one of the most common problems you'll find is that you just can't sit down for long enough. This is another thing that can only really be fixed with practice and determination. Tell yourself that you've got to stick to it for at least a month.

After this time you'll find it much easier, and you'll be able to sit still for long periods of time.

4: It hurts my knees or back

If you're in pain, you should stop. Meditation shouldn't hurt at all, and if it does, you should stop until it doesn't hurt. Try taking it slowly, and making sure that when you set yourself up for meditation, you're not sitting in a way that might get uncomfortable after a few minutes. This takes a bit of practice to get to the point where you can tell what's going to be uncomfortable before doing it.

You want to get to the point where you can sort of 'sense' what position is going to be uncomfortable, before getting into it. The best position is just the cross legged sitting position on a cushion or something like that, with a straight back and your chest out.

For 90% of people, there will be literally no problems with this position. But for some people, maybe people with back pain or posture issues, this might be a problem. Just take it at your own pace and find what works for you.

It's going to be different for everyone. If it hurts your knees, because sitting cross legged is hard for you, then find something to sit on like a bench that doesn't have a back. A good place to find something like this is just a park or somewhere outside.

By sitting with your back straight and with nothing supporting your back, you force yourself to be aware of what you're doing and think about what you're doing. This makes it easier to meditate, and stops you falling asleep.

5: I don't have time!

Ah, time. The classic default excuse for almost everything. I don't have time. It's been said that if you don't have time to meditate, you need it more than anyone else.

Everyone has time to meditate, and if you don't, you can make time. It only takes a few minutes a day and if you're saying 'I don't even have 5 spare minutes in my day' then just get up 5 minutes earlier.

I find it very hard to believe that a person doesn't have even 5 minutes spare in their day, but even if that were the case, just move things around so you do..

Or just get up 5 minutes earlier. It's not going to make a difference if you wake up 5 minutes earlier, and it means you can set yourself up for the day more easily. In fact, I would suggest meditating first thing in the morning for most people.

This is when I find it has the biggest effect. It sets me up for the day and makes everything else easier.

But it's also been said that meditation GIVES you more time than it takes away. This is because it makes you more alert and aware during the other things you're doing with your day. So if you don't think you have time, think again!

6: Nothing's happening

You've been sitting there for ten minutes, your timers gone off but nothing's happened. What's wrong? Are you doing it wrong? You start to question why you bothered buying this book or even thinking about learning how to meditate. don't worry, this happens a lot.

A lot of people expect that meditation is some mystical thing and that by doing it, they'll experience a 'breakthrough moment', where everything in the universe makes sense and they feel at one with everything. It doesn't work like that sadly.

You will feel better but it's a slow process. Sure, it CAN happen instantly, and I know the first time I meditated, I did feel instantly better but it's not that way for everyone. For lots of people, meditation can be difficult to learn and unusual to experience.

But like I said, press on through that, and you'll get massive benefits. But don't look for an event or an instant moment where it feels 'different'. This is the fastest way to burn out and stop performing the practice, because you don't think it's 'working'. It is working, but you've just got to give it more time.

So those are the most common problems people have. If you've had one or more of those problems when trying to meditate, please keep going.

Don't worry about it. Of course, if you've experienced a problem like pain or something, just adjust the way you're sitting and make sure you're not in any sort of pain. But most of the problems you'll have will be the mental ones.

Things like not being able to sit still long enough or not being able to concentrate on what you're doing. Those only get easier with time and practice, so just keep going with them!

How to practice this every day

This needs to be practiced literally every single day.

Of course you can miss a day here and there, but the main benefits are mainly felt when you practice this every day for about 60 days or so.

There are a few ways of doing that. You need to firstly set yourself a challenge to meditate every day for 60 days. You can write a chart or tick off days on a calendar that you've meditated, if that makes it easier.

I like to use a journal or notepad and just write down the date, and how the meditation went. Of course I only really did that at the start, to build the habit.

Once the habit is built, it's very hard to NOT meditate. I feel very strange and uncomfortable if I DON'T meditate in the morning now. It really sets me up for the day and helps me to focus on what I'm doing.

But there's one thing that's very important to remember:

Meditating once per day for 3 minutes is much easier than meditating once a week for an HOUR.

This really needs to be a daily thing. If you can only commit to doing about 3 minutes a day, that's fine but make sure it literally is every single day.

Ideally, you want to be meditating for about 20-30 minutes a day every day. This can be spread out into 15 minutes in the morning and 15 in the evening. Or, you could even meditate for 10 minutes in the morning, 10 before lunch and 10 before bed.

However you break it up, the key is to get a certain number of minutes per DAY not per week.

It really only changes the brain if you do it every day, and it's not something like emails that you can just bunch up to the end of the week, and reply to them all then. You can't 'binge meditate' at the weekend!

It's every damn day.

When you're first starting, you need to do it every day and do it somewhere quiet. By finding somewhere quiet, you limit the distractions that you'd otherwise get. Quiet places are much better for meditation so don't try and do this in a busy cafe or on the bus or something like that.

There's not really an secret for how to do this every day. You've just got to set the target and do it. After all, it's YOU that's got everything to gain here, so just ask yourself 'Do I want to meditate and feel better?'.

But even on days when you don't really feel like it, it's important to do it then too. If you don't feel like meditating, you often need it more THEN than on other days, so always meditate.

If you're having a really bad day and you just don't want to meditate, THAT'S when it's needed the most. It's needed most then because it will make you feel better! It's literally MEANT to make you feel better during those bad days, so always do it.

From now on, make sure to meditate using that technique at least once a day, every single day. From this point on, we're going to talk about some other types of meditation and techniques, but you don't need to learn these.

Spiritual meditation

You've already learned all you need to know about meditation, and it's now just up to you to actually practice it every single day, every morning.

Chapter 2: Spiritual Meditation

Meditation finds its roots mainly in religion and spirituality although like we said, you don't HAVE to be religious to meditate. Regardless of which culture you look at, it tends to originate from the process of seeking enlightenment, connection, God, and wisdom.

Most people think of Buddhist monks when they think of meditation: bald and simply clothed, cross-legged on a bare floor mouthing "om"s with eyes closed. It's true, this is one way to meditate. However, there are many others.

Meditation can still be used for this traditional purpose, regardless of your personal beliefs. In the Western world, it is most commonly practiced as a part of Buddhism or Hindu, a function of Christianity, or a ritualistic aspect of Islam.

Their approaches tended to differ based on the teachings of their prophets and spiritual leaders or teachers, but over time some similarities have arisen.

Meditating on Spiritual Guidance

Firstly, meditation can be done a number of ways. One of the things you can do is to increase your spiritual guidance and focus on a particular thing or idea.

Of course this CAN be used for religions.

You can focus on a particular prayer or idea but this can be applied to any person with any beliefs. If you're trying to instil ANY belief in your mind for example 'I will become rich', you must meditate on it and BELIEVE it.

If you are looking to grow in your understanding, you might select something you have so far failed to comprehend, or wish you better understood. If you wish to find more joy in your beliefs, you might select a Psalm or other acclamation of praise.

If instead you wish to overcome a temptation that is distancing you from your higher power, you may choose a verse or saying that relates to what you are working on.

Choose a quiet place. Fortunately, this can be one of the easiest types of meditation to start. It requires you replace your thoughts, rather than try to avert them completely. You may wish to start by relaxing using one of the physical or visualization meditations explained later in this book. When you feel you have sufficiently let go of other thoughts or tensions, begin repeating the words you have chosen.

Repeat them slowly, contemplating each word. Pay attention to how each word sounds. Visualize the words in your head. Look at how the meaning changes if you rearrange them.

You may be tempted to try to relate your chosen phrase to other ideas, but focus only on the small portion you have chosen. Start by doing this for a very short time, perhaps a few minutes, then slowly increase your time.

Meditating on an Idea or Moral

Often it is beneficial to focus on aspects of spiritual wellness to grow. This may be a goal you have, like to give up an indulgence that damages your spiritual practices. It may instead be a mantra that brings you better into alignment and focus on your desire to improve.

As before, begin by focusing on that which you wish to change. Phrase this idea in the positive: that you will do as you will in this improved spiritual state.

Focus on the idea.

Visualize yourself successfully practicing your change. Believe you feel the change within yourself as you grow, the warmth and rightness. In this, you are teaching your mind to do this new will and feel it natural and right, a normal part of your daily life.

This is an example of how you can use meditation to focus on an idea and think about a particular thing you want to change. Say if you want to quit smoking, for example.

You can tell yourself 'I am NOT a smoker' and meditate on that phrase over and over again. After a while of doing that, you really will believe it and you'll start to change your behaviour to match that statement and that belief.

This is a powerful example of how you use basic words and repetition to change your beliefs.

Like we've said, meditation is really just about FOCUS. Focus on your breath, or in this case focused an idea or statement.

You can use it to create beliefs or change your existing beliefs on yourself. Most people don't use it for this though, and instead just use it to focus on the breathe and feeling better.

Meditation in
MOTION

Chapter 3: Meditation in Motion

The Beginnings of Moving Meditation

While most people do not think of meditation as energetic, or lively, it truly can be. You don't NEED to be sitting down with your eyes closed to meditate.

For centuries, if not millennia, the movements of the body have been used as a form of meditation and in tandem with other forms of meditation. In the East, yoga has been used as a spiritual practice of growth and learning, balance and centering.

It has been popularized today as a form of exercise to limber up and increase flexibility, but originally it was intimately related to meditation and spirituality, and still is for true practitioners. That's right, yoga is a form of meditation, just like many other types of movement and exercise.

In many Middle Eastern and African countries, dance has been used as a spiritual conduit and meditative practice, drawing on the positions and rhythms of the body to train the mind.

Another long-standing type of moving meditation is part of the pilgrimage, or visit to a holy place. The long walk to visit a place of spiritual power was not only about the destination, but about the actual act of walking itself. Similarly, the repetitive act of swimming, with its otherworldly environs, carries a meditative power all its own.

Of course, the physical motions of ritual prayer are also a kind of meditation. This is a practice found in every religious system around the world, although it is more marked in some than others.

So you can actually meditate while doing something else.

So the excuse of 'I don't have time' is even less valid! In fact, sometimes it's EASIER to meditate when doing something repetitive like cycling or walking, because you have something physical to focus on that isn't just your breath. If you're walking, for example you can just focus on your footsteps.

Of course you still have to focus on not thinking or interacting with the thoughts and things around you. It can be a bit tempting when you're walking and meditating to just look at the details of the things around you and interact with them, to ask yourself questions about what you're seeing and entertain all these thoughts in your head.

But that defeats the point of meditation.

If you find it hard to meditate while sitting down in your room, you might be be ready for waking meditation just yet. If you're reading this and you STILL can't meditate properly, please go back to the first meditation tutorial and re-read it until you understand it. Also make sure to practice it every day.

How to Practice Moving Meditation

Yoga as Meditation

Yoga is possibly the easiest example of moving meditation. It can be readily accessible, as classes and yoga studios exist almost everywhere. In order to use yoga as a form of meditation, begin by taking deep, steadying breaths before beginning. Know your body, and extend your awareness to every part of it- each limb, finger, organ and breath.

As you begin to move, maintain this bodily awareness.

Feel how your hands press together, or into the mat. Notice the fluid ways in which your muscles contract and release as you change positions. Feel the tensions as you hold poses, and note how your breathing affects how each position and movement feels. Do so to the exclusion of noticing anything else. Feel it all.

As with other types of meditation, repeated practice improves the quality of your meditations. A good place to start is a basic sun salutation.

These are typically only a few positions, completed in a circuit several times with measured, matching breathing. Use these repetitions to train your body and mind to focus only on its own movements.

Walking as Meditation

While the act of pilgrimage has faded in many places, a different type of walking meditation has arisen. Possibly best known of these is the phenomenon of "Thru-hiking." a thru-hike consists of travelling by foot over a long distance on a trail or path, living off of the land or from a backpack.

It is strangely comforting to many to be so simplified, with only the necessities of survival. It is also hard not to approach a meditative pitch while hiking in this way.

There is nothing but the hiker, the steps following one after another rhythmically, the attention to the path for sure footing, and the surrounding nature.

Even in foul weather, the lack of rushing stimuli found in the outside world creates a meditative state in even the most experienced walker. This one is both easy and hard to practice. It is easy, as it requires only walking.

It is hard, as it requires physical fitness, time, and supplies. Be sure you are well educated before attempting this type of meditation. However, the constant immersive nature of this meditation has a powerful effect on those who complete it.

Many people become dismayed or fearful when they get to the end of the trail, where many would expect them to be excited to reach their goal. The magic of a thru-hike lies in the walking itself, and the journey, not the destination. It can be a transformative experience that alters one's worldview for a lifetime.

But that's all very intense, right?

Well, you can actually meditate just while walking around town! Or if you're walking your dog, you can meditate while walking. It's very simple, just focus on your footsteps.

That's it. Just don't think about anything, and just like normal meditation, when you REALISE you're thinking about something else, just bring your awareness back to your body and back to the footsteps.

Meditation by Swimming and Dancing

Using swimming or dancing to practice meditation draws on the power of other forces, just as walking draws on the power of nature and repetition. Swimming gains meditative "oomph" from the lulling nature of water.

It mutes sounds, softens the feel of the skin and body as it moves, making one lighter in his or her own body. Dance draws a person into music and community, things which have long had the power to change both mind and heart.

The key to using these things as forms of meditation is in the focus and intent. When swimming or dancing, establish a cadence and repetition. Breathe every third stroke, and keep a measured pace. Focus ONLY on the water against your skin, and the feel of the movements, excluding other thoughts.

When dancing, the same thing applies. Let go of outside thoughts. Allow yourself to be immersed in the music, and keep a simple rhythm and repetition to your movements, focusing on the feel of your body as you do so. Enjoy the effort you are making in your movements.

You might have already experienced this feeling of being in the 'zone' when running, jogging or on a treadmill. I've had several moments in the gym where I've been meditating while walking or jogging on a cross trainer or something like that, and I haven't noticed an hour go by. I just get into the zone and deeply meditate.

This shows that you can actually meditate even if you're NOT physically relaxed. Meditation refers mainly to the act of focusing on only one thing for a certain period of time, and it can be done almost anywhere.

Effects of Moving Meditation

Moving meditation has the added benefit of healing and growing the body as well as the mind and heart. It can increase one's comfort with the body and all its eccentricities, making it a familiar home rather than something to be managed or tamed.

It increases strength and resilience, and adds the release of endorphins to the peace and joy brought about by all meditation.

You might have experienced the 'runners high' that people report. The feeling of intense joy and happiness about halfway through a run when you're flooded with endorphins, you've maybe been in a meditative state without realising it, and you're just HAPPY.

Most valuable, perhaps, is the creation of a mind-body union that is often lost in a busy life, or when surrounded by a society that sees the body as something separate from the mind, to be controlled. It is valuable to know that body, mind, and spirit are one.

There are some powerful effects of moving meditation.

I think the most important thing to focus on is just the ACT of doing whatever you're doing. Be more aware of the thing you're doing. If you're running, focus only on the footsteps and breathing.

If you're cycling, just focus on the peddling. And let everything else, all the thoughts, emotions and feelings just let them flow over you and out of your awareness.

Running is said to be damaging to your knees, and from experience I know this is true. I can't honestly recommend that you start running, but swimming and cycling I can suggest you do. In particular, cycling while listening to some meditation audio is a great thing.

Visualisation
METHODS

Chapter 4: Visualization Methods

Common Applications of Visualization as Meditation

Historically, visualization has been used as part of spiritual growth and connection to a higher power or to the oneness of the universe. Recently, it has also gained recognition as a valuable tool in treating mental illness. It is a thoroughly researched technique often taught to patients in CBT (Cognitive Behavioral Therapy).

It can greatly improve the quality of life for those with depression and anxiety. It is also often used in different ways to treat trauma and PTSD (Post-Traumatic Stress Disorder).

The two main ways that visualization is used are in recreating traumatic events and responding to them in healthy ways, so as to take away their power; and in creating a safe space involving all the senses that can be a kind of refuge during particularly challenging bouts of symptoms, including panic attacks.

How to Practice Visualization Meditation

Personal Growth and Goals

As with spiritual growth, visualization of success often creates the capacity for success. This is a more advanced form of meditation by the way. By visualising what you WANT in your life, you'll be able to easily get it if you put in the work.

But it all starts with visualising what you want. If you don't KNOW what you want, how can you expect to get it?

You have to take a few minutes or hours even, to work out what you REALLY want. And not just money. Most of us think we want money but we really just want what we think the money will GET us.

Maybe it's being able to sit on a beach, or go climbing mountains, right? Well, you can get those things with a lot less money than you think, so focus on what you actually WANT. If it's really money, then that's fine too, just focus on a specific AMOUNT of money and a deadline too. Tell yourself something like 'I'll earn XX amount of money before X date'.

And meditation can massively help you visualise the things you want, and help you focus on getting them.

To practice this type of meditation, start by finding a comfortable place to sit or lay. Close your eyes and decide what it is you want to achieve. Fully believe you can do so, pushing out feelings of doubt. Instead, visualize yourself achieving the goal.

Bring it to life in great detail, drawing on all five of your senses.

Do this regularly as you work toward your goal. The more you do this, the easier it will be. When you doubt what you are doing or waver in your efforts to achieve your goal, draw up this visualization and follow it through again.

Don't forget to include the ways it will affect different areas of your life, including your own health or happiness. Believing you can do something, or that something will come to pass, creates powerful intentions that change the way you behave.

When I look at my life the last few years, my life has become an almost EXACT manifestation of the goals and visualisations I did 3 years ago.

So close that it's almost scary actually, and now I'm thinking 'Why didn't I set BIGGER goals al those years ago!?'. So now I regularly review my goals and try and push myself to visualise and achieve bigger things.

But your life will literally become a product of what you plan for and which goals you set yourself. If your goals are specific make sure they're really what you want, because you'll GET the goals you set yourself! You'll get those results.

Treating Anxiety and Depression

Visualization is also a powerful tool to fight anxiety and depression.

It can slow a racing mind, replace false or painful thoughts, and provide a safe place from the attacks of an unwell mind. For instance, it can create a place where intrusive thoughts, the hurtful negative thoughts that spring seemingly unbidden into the mind of the affected person, cannot easily enter.

To practice this type of meditation, find a comfortable place to sit or lay. Close your eyes and breathe deeply. It may help to count your breaths, slowing them and making them even.

Now, think of a place that you have been when younger, where you were happy or peaceful. It should be the kind of place that allows you to feel safe, peaceful, loved, and calm. Recreate that place in your mind's eye.

Start by seeing what it looks like. Be very detailed, including the time of day, season, color of the sky or wallpaper, and so on. Include all of your senses, drawing up what it feels like when you touch a nearby tree or a couch. Feel on your skin the breeze or the warmth.

Taste the air around you, and hear the music or the rustling of leaves. Now, hold this place in your mind. Be there fully. Stay in that state as long as you are able.

To start with, you likely will only be able to do this for a few seconds or minutes, and you might need quiet or a very peaceful location to do so.

But over time, you will be able to draw up this place and be there readily, even when you are stressed or hurting. In this way, you can create for yourself a safe place to be when you need space from your thoughts and feelings to recuperate.

It's a very powerful psychological technique you can use to go back into a relaxed state, and you should use this in the future if you have depressed days or you're feeling down.

Another powerful way of creating this sense of happiness and purpose is to create a vision board. I know this might sound like it's a bit unrelated to meditation, but I'll bring it back round, I promise.

A vision board is a collection of words and images that make you have an EMOTIONAL and motivated reaction when you look at it. I like to collect pictures of the lifestyle I want, the places I want to go and see, and the type of person I want to become. This might include role models, travel inspiration photos from Instagram, or just a random mixture of things.

It's going to be different for everyone, but here's what you do.

You create a physical board that you put on your wall with the images using a cork board or by sticking them with sellotape.

Every morning, take 5 minutes to stare at your board and get inspired and motivated. Then, close your eyes and IMAGINE what it would be like to live the life you DREAM of living. Literally feel it and visualise it vividly with all of your senses.

My vision for the future is so vivid and clearly defined, I can almost touch it, and when you get to that point, nothing can stop you.

You'll be able to almost reach out and touch you dream life, and with that sort of purpose and drive, you'll get to those goals. You'll be very surprised how effective just meditating and visualising your goals really can be.

Relaxation and Release Methods

Some visualization techniques are simple and draw on other meditative techniques as well. One of these is the visualization of cleansing the soul. In this practice, start as with the others, comfortable and with the eyes closed. It is a valuable tool for letting go of a racing mind when trying to sleep, so you may be laying on your back.

You should be able to breathe deeply and easily. Start by pacing your breathing, slowly inhaling deeply then exhaling slowly.

Visualize the anxiety or strain within yourself as something you identify as a "poison." Some find it helpful to think of it as a purple vapor or black gas. Similarly, picture out in the world goodness and peace as something else, perhaps gold liquid.

As you breathe out, picture the bad inside you exiting with your breathe as that vapor and incinerating as it hits the air. As you breathe in, picture the golden goodness filling the space left by the bad that has left.

Do so slowly, releasing it from every part of your body until none of the bad is left and you are full of the good. This will increase feelings of peace and wellness. If you are seeking sleep, it will relax you and allow you to go to sleep with a calm mind.

Another visualization is to picture stress as a physical object within your body. Most people with stress, anxiety or depression identify physical manifestations of it within themselves, often as a tight chest, heavy head, or leaden weight.

Picture these feelings as physical objects. Perhaps they are tumors, or lead weights, or pieces of fire. Then, visualize another object destroying the first. Perhaps the immune system simply breaks down the object, removing it.

Perhaps the same golden light as before enters in, destroying it into smoke that quickly dissipates. Finding a set of visualized objects which best represent the feelings and experiences may take time, but will be more effective the longer they are used.

Benefits of These Practices

Using these types of visualization practices benefits a person in many ways. Often feelings of anxiety or stress decrease overall, regardless of the time of day or night. The visualization acts as a pressure valve, lowering the level at any given time.

Similarly, this type of visualization can be completed in only a few minutes if needed, acting as an emergency stop on painful feelings. These kinds of practices are often incorporated into professional mental health treatments because of their power and accessibility.

Practicing visualization meditation before bed can increase quality of sleep, resulting in a well-rested mind capable of healthier thoughts. During the day, it can reduce the energy of negative feelings, allowing one to relax and use the energy in more efficient and useful ways.

Finally, these types of meditation create a sense of peace and wellness that is often lost when someone is battling a mental illness. Recovering access to these positive feelings can create faith in the future and buffer progress in trauma treatment, especially after painful recreations and processing sessions.

Verbalisation Methods

Chapter 5: Verbalization Meditation

Verbalization as a form a of meditation originated in the Eastern practices of Buddhism and Hindu. The key difference lies in that while single-syllable meditation most commonly occurred in Buddhist practices, Hindi practices frequently used phrases or mantras.

This is not to say they exist only in these practices, but that they primarily occurred there, while showing up less frequently elsewhere.

These could be in the simplest form of meditation as a focus on nothingness or on one aspect of spirituality, or they could be more complex, bordering on the common modern practice of daily affirmation.

This is where lost of people get confused or lost. The act of chanting or repeating a word or sound is not a weird one. I think a lot of people just don't understand it or know why people do it, and so it gets labeled as that 'crazy meditation thing' and people stay away.

It doesn't have to be strange and confusing.

How to Practice Verbalization as Meditation

Single Syllable Verbalization

In order to practice single syllable meditation, it is important again to find a quiet place to sit comfortably and peacefully, without disturbance. While it is a great simplification of meaning, one would do well to start by choosing from the three syllables om, ah, and hum.

Om refers loosely to the body. Ah refers, equally loosely, to speech. And Hum refers to the mind. These correlations are generalizations, and can be furthered when the meditation practicer is prepared to do so. Choose one of these to meditate on, as it calls to you.

Once you have chosen a syllable, begin breathing deeply and evenly, taking the same slow measure of breath in as you breathe out. Once your breathing is regular, begin using your exhale to verbalize the syllable you have chosen.

Think of the syllable as round, neither emphasizing the beginning or end but evenly moving through the sound. When a sense of calm or peace has entered into the practice, lengthen the period of exhale in relation to the inhale, so that the exhalation and verbalization last twice as long as the inhalation.

However, no part of each breath cycle should be hurried. Focus only on the syllable and the way it reverberates in the chest and diaphragm.

Interestingly, the word 'Om' comes from Sanskrit and means 'I am that'. It stems from the belief that we're all one with the universe and all connected.

This doesn't mean you have to give it that meaning though. It can be easily used as a way of focusing on your breath.

Mantra or Phrase Meditation

The basic application of this type of meditation, is similar to the single syllable meditation. However, a phrase, single-sentence prayer, or mantra is said during the exhalation. Begin by sitting comfortably in a quiet place without disruptions. Start breathing deeply and evenly. Once this feels calm and natural, begin stating your phrase as you exhale.

You might consider any monks you have heard meditate, regardless of their religion, as they provide a good model for how this should be performed.

The words should be said evenly, without undue emphasis on any given word or syllable, and without variation in intonation or volume. The whole sentence is even and paced. Repeat the phrase every time you exhale.

Verbal Meditation with Others

Practicing the above types of verbal meditation on its own is a powerful practice. However, completing these meditations with others creates a unity and strength of conviction not achieved alone.

To do so, it is important that all those participating are in agreement on the method and duration of practice.

It can be useful to have one person whom all others follow in pacing, or added music or signifying instrument to time verbalizations. Choose the syllable or phrase to be repeated, and the length of time it will be done. Some people prefer to seat themselves in a way that removes the temptation of looking at the others involved.

Start the music or timing by which each verbalization will be completed. Those meditating together should endeavor to say each syllable or word with the same intonation, speed and pitch as others.

Meditating to Music or Sounds

A traditional approach to verbalized meditation is to verbalize along with a music instrument. One traditional option is a gong, drum, or other single-note instrument.

When the instrument sounds once, breathe in. When it sounds again, breathe out. When the pace feels natural, begin verbalizing along with the timing of the notes.

This type of verbalization works well for those with anxiety or self-esteem difficulties, as it calms the body physically and mentally and fosters a strong sense of well-being.

Awareness meditation

Chapter 6: Awareness Meditation

Mindfulness Over Time

"Mindfulness" is a popular buzzword as of late. At its most basic, mindfulness simply means being truly aware of each part of every moment. When you eat dinner, you are aware of the flavor, texture, smells and consistency of each bite.

When working, every part of the task fully absorbs one's attention. Over time, as the speed of life increases, the commonality of mindfulness decreases.

Modern society tends to value multitasking, and only lately realized the impact this has on personal well-being. Immersion in each task has its own value and reward, even in something as small as washing dishes.

Mindfulness is simple to practice on the surface, but true application on a regular basis requires effort and focus. In fact, mindfulness is sometimes called "the meditation of focus".

It can be difficult to apply in all areas of life, especially when society expects speed and a constant state of "being on." Mindfulness means one must reject this standard of being in favor of a slower pace. Of course, beyond the personal health benefits, one result of mindfulness is typically increased quality of work in lieu of decreased quantity.

It literally is just about being aware of everything you're doing, even if it seems small or unimportant to you like washing the dishes. This awareness will help you be more aware and mindful in your life.

A Powerful Mindfulness Exercise

One common way to practice mindfulness takes only a few minutes and a place to lay down. Starting with your toes, tense all of the muscles in all ten toes.

Hold them tight for a count of ten, then release the tension and allow them to relax. Move up to the muscles of your calves, and repeat. Do the same with your thighs, then your buttocks.

Start again with your fingers, making a fist with each hand and clenching it tight before releasing. Continue by tensing and releasing your forearms, then your upper arms. Next, flex and hold your abdominal muscles and release.

Do the same with your shoulders and chest. Finally, tense and release your neck and the muscles of your face.

As you practice this technique, focus your mind on the feeling of the tensing and releasing in the muscle group as you do it. The result is a feeling of physical and emotional relaxation.

Another mindfulness endeavor is similarly enjoyable in its simplicity. Find a quiet place where you can be undisturbed for a few minutes. Get a handful of a simple snacks, like sunflower kernels, popped corn, or peanuts.

Start by looking at the (for example) popcorn pieces. In your mind, describe the kernels with as many detail words as you can. Then look at the popcorn a minute longer, doing your best not to think in words, instead absorbing the appearance. Next, close your eyes.

Bring a single piece of popcorn to your nose and smell it gently. Breathe deeply, doing your best to maintain the thoughtless momentum you began a moment before. Next, put the popcorn piece in your mouth.

Chew it slowly, paying attention to the texture, the flavor, and the way it changes in consistency. Repeat this with each of the pieces of popcorn in your hand. This exercise embodies the hallmark awareness of mindfulness.

I know this might sound a bit silly, especially if you get found just sniffing popcorn with your eyes closed, but it's important to start to be aware of your feelings and body more.

Take in the information your senses are giving you and making the most of it. Life is all about these small moments, and if we can learn to be aware and happy in the small moments, well that's all that really matters.

Daily Applications

To take this a step further, start seeking to be as deeply aware of everything in life as of those popcorn pieces. Notice the smell of the dust stirred up in the wind from the street. Feel the heat of the sun when first starting the car. Hear the murmured chatter mingling with the sounds of steel in the subway.

Mindfulness applies to actions as well. When working, give full attention to the task at hand, neither looking back or forward in time.

Release feelings of frustration and accept what needs done as the thing to do now, and nothing else. This kind of focus calms the mind, rather than winding it up with "should, would, could".

Of course, mindfulness can adopt an even higher meaning when applied to relationships. Being fully aware of those around, whether they are a close part of life or not, lends a richness to life not easily found. Focus fully on the needs and details of those in your life.

Why Mindfulness Is IMPORTANT!

Practicing mindfulness allows a person to fully appreciate each part of life in its entirety, making life more worth living.

When each detail stands out, gratitude is almost unavoidable, and certainly much more attainable. The peace which accompanies mindfulness is proven by research to lower the incidence of depressive action, anxiety, chronic stress and panic attacks. Surely it is something worth investing time and energy into learning.

Bonus tips and tools

Chapter 7: Bonus tools and tricks

This section is more just to give you a few bonus tips and tools, things that have helped me meditate over the years, and hopefully will help you. You don't have to get these things or practice these tips, but I find them very useful.

By the way, we're at the end of the book now but it's only the start of your journey. Meditation can unlock many different things for you, and it will take care of you like nothing else can.

In the good times and during the bad, meditation will see you through. I know for a fact that on the journey of building my business and achieving my dream life I would've imploded if I hadn't been meditating.

It really does make all the difference and I think it has the potential to change the entire world for the better. Combine meditation with eating a plant based diet, sleeping right and doing things that inspire you? And you've got a pretty awesome life.

How to build meditation into your life

To actually build this into your life, you'll need to first build the habit. The habit is the most important part because without the habit you'll just meditate when you 'feel like it' which could be rarely.

It's important to do it when you don't feel like it, especially when you first start. It's a great habit to build and it's NEVER going to make your life WORSE, so what do you have to lose? Just be strict with yourself and make time every day to meditate and be mindful.

I've found that it's very useful to combine meditation with other habits, to make them ALL easier to maintain. Things like waking up early, writing in a journal or working on my goals, it's easier when you bunch these habits together.

I think the official name for this is 'habit stacking' but you can call it what you want. The fact is that by bunching several good habits together, you're much more likely to do them all.

If you've already written in a journal, done a bit of exercise and done some reading, how can you

NOT also do your meditation? It's part of your routine and it's just easier to do it than it is to NOT do it. That's where you want to aim for.

Tools and tips for practicing meditation

Don't be too hard on yourself: It's easy to be hard on yourself when you first start. This is actually part of the fight or flight reaction in play really. Your mind says 'you can't meditate, look how terrible you are!

You should feel terrible!'. And you start to put yourself down. Try and ignore that and just tell yourself that it's meant to be hard at the start, it just takes practice to get better.

Don't give up: It's so easy to give up if it doesn't 'work' after the first week or so. Don't do that, I can PROMISE you the benefits on the other side of 60 days are well worth the wait. And it might even happen much faster than that, just build it into your daily routine!

Just do one type: There are lots of types of meditation and lots of ways you could do it. It's important to focus on only one type like the main breathing meditation I taught you first. That's all you need to do. If after a few months of doing that, you feel like improving it or doing something different then fine but don't overwhelm yourself too soon. Like I said, I personally just use that method because it's the most effective, and it gets me the results I want.

Using binaural beats to meditate

Binaural beats are a special type of sound wave that you can use to reach deeper levels of meditation in your practice. The way they work is like this:

Two slightly different frequencies of sound are played, one in each ear.

Because your brain can't experience the tiny difference in frequency, it sort of 'creates' a frequency for itself which is a mixture of the two different frequencies. This happens in the brain and by doing that, your brain enters a different brainwave state.

It's sort of like a tuning fork which slowly movs your brain into a certain pitch or frequency of brainwaves.

And the effects of that are profound.

It means that by listening to different binaural beats and frequencies you can decide which brainwave state to put yourself in. Pretty powerful, right? You can have binaural beats that move you into a focused state, relaxed, sleepy, energetic, you name it.

They're really amazing, and you can use them to do all sorts of crazy things like focusing better, studying for longer, and indeed meditating for longer and deeper.

This effect is widely known in the personal development world and there are lots of audio tracks you can buy. I would suggest buying them, because the binaural beats you'll find on YouTube are often not real, don't work or are very bad quality.

I've been using binaural beats for a number of years, and they're great. I find they're able to get me into a deeper state of relaxation and meditation with almost no effort.

They're particularly good for meditating in the early hours of the morning. Because your brain is already in the right frame of mind for meditation, you're able to 'jump' into a deep meditative state very easily by listening to some binaural beats.

You can find the best binaural beats listed on <u>our Resources page here</u>, and we've reviewed the main ones too. On that page I list the main binaural beats I personally use to meditate and feel better.

Special free bonus for book readers

I've created a special page on my website where I share free tutorials, life hacking tips, personal development resources and all sorts of discounts on things that I've secured for you guys. To see the discounts and tutorials, enter this URL in your browser:

<u>https://www.TranscendYourLimits.com/ Bonus/</u>

+++

If you take nothing else from this book, just make sure you meditate every single day, even if it's just for 3 minutes.

You'll look back on your life and how you FEEL in a few months and be amazed at the new life you've created.

+++

Made in the USA
Columbia, SC
17 July 2019